THEN & NOW®

DOWNTOWN BOSTON

This December 1950 photograph shows Boston's Downtown Crossing thronged with a multitude of shoppers who stream in all directions from Winter, Summer, and Washington Streets. Filene's department store, designed by noted Chicago architect Daniel Burnham and built in 1912, is seen in the center with a monumental decorated Christmas tree placed above the corner of its awning. On the far right is a corner of Jordan Marsh department store, designed by Winslow & Wetherall, with its Summer Street addition built in 1948 by Perry, Shaw, and Hepburn (now known as Macy's). The spire of the Old South Church can be seen in the distance at the corner of Washington and Milk Streets. Today, this intersection is known as Downtown Crossing and is designated as a pedestrian area with numerous pushcarts and outdoor seating that attracts both shoppers and tourists alike.

THEN & NOW®

DOWNTOWN BOSTON

Anthony Mitchell Sammarco
Contemporary Photographs by James Z. Kyprianos

ARCADIA
PUBLISHING

Published by Arcadia Publishing
Charleston, South Carolina

Printed in the United States of America

Library of Congress Catalog Card Number: 2002110442

Then and Now is a registered trademark and is used under license from
Salamander Books Limited

For all general information contact Arcadia Publishing at:
Telephone 843-853-2070
Fax 843-853-0044
E-mail sales@arcadiapublishing.com
For customer service and orders:
Toll-Free 1-888-313-2665

Visit us on the Internet at www.arcadiapublishing.com

Franklin Street was laid out in 1798 as a gently curving street between Washington and India Streets. On the right was the Tontine Crescent, a 240-foot row designed by noted architect Charles Bulfinch (1763–1844) and built between 1793–1795 as the first connected brick row houses in Boston. Designed with eight brick houses flanking an impressive pedimented center pavilion, the row houses shared a uniform roofline, neoclassical details, and color—a stone gray painted to emulate Portland stone with white painted trim. The design included four duplex houses across the street facing a tree-planted square, which spawned the widespread use of treelined squares throughout the city in the 19th century. On the left are brick duplexes, and the spire of the Federal Street Church, also designed by Bulfinch and built in 1809, can be seen just above the trees. (Courtesy Boston Athenaeum.)

CONTENTS

Downtown Boston, seen from the air just following World War II, had the customhouse tower as its only skyscraper dominating the skyline. The tower was built in 1915 from designs by the noted architectural firm of Peabody & Stearns, with the tower surmounting the original Greek Revival customhouse designed by Ammi Burnham Young and built of Quincy granite between 1837 and 1849 at the head of Long Wharf. Throughout the 19th century, the area of Boston's waterfront was expanded into Boston Harbor through infilling, with the new lands promptly being developed for commercial structures. In the foreground is the Northern Avenue Bridge. Designed by engineer William Jackson and built in 1910, it crosses the Fort Point Channel and connects the city proper and South Boston in an area known as Fort Point. Today, the Southeast Expressway, which cut a wide swathe through this area, is being dismantled and a greenstrip will shortly replace the onetime green metal monster. The former customhouse has been converted to an elegant timeshare of the Marriott Corporation known as Marriott's Custom House.

INTRODUCTION

No man who consents to the destruction of an ancient building has any right to pretend that he cares about art. or has any excuse to plead in defence of his crime against civilization and progress save sheer brutal ignorance.

—William Morris

Boston was settled in 1630 by a group of Puritans from England who were seeking religious freedom, as well as liberty, from the oppressive policies of Charles I. They created in the New World a "city upon a hill." Initially called Shawmut, the Massachusetts Indian name that is supposed to have meant a spring of water, the town was also referred to as Trimount, an acknowledgment of the three hills later to become known as Mount Vernon, Beacon, and Pemberton Hills. Trimount was later corrupted as Tremont by both spelling and pronunciation, and a street perpetuates it today. In September1630, the Puritans officially called their settlement Boston, after Boston in Lincolnshire, England. When settled, the town was an 800-acre land mass that was connected to the mainland at Roxbury by a narrow strip of land that became known as the Neck. This area, which was to be infilled and developed in the 19th century as the present South End of Boston, is the current area of Washington Street.

In the first two centuries (1630–1830) after the peninsula was settled by the Puritans, Boston saw the laying out of streets, the building of houses, and the erection of places of worship. It also observed the development of the waterfront with wharves that projected into Boston Harbor, a move that increased Boston's mercantile economy. Beginning with the turn of the 19th century, the town was to see tremendous topographical changes over the next five decades, especially the leveling of the three hills and the infilling of such areas as the Dock Square and Long Wharf. These areas became the site of Quincy Market and the Boston Custom House, each of which signified the development of the city's commercial aspects.

Boston was incorporated as a city by its citizens on March 4, 1822, after which it saw tremendous growth under the first three mayors: John Phillips (1822), Josiah Quincy (1823–1828), and Harrison Gray Otis (1829–1831). These three men would see to it that Boston was perceived as not just the "Athens of America," but as Oliver Wendell Holmes called it, the "Hub of the Universe." Though much of the old South End, the area of present-day Downtown Boston, was one of the most architecturally elegant sections of any city on the eastern seaboard, it was rapidly changing. By the time of the Civil War, the formerly residential streets, such as Summer, High, Pearl, and Franklin Streets had given way to commerce and were being rebuilt with four- and five-story commercial blocks that changed the character of the city. However, all of this rapid development came to an abrupt halt due to the mass devastation wrought by the Great Boston Fire of November 9–10, 1872. The fire destroyed 40 acres of the downtown business area and wreaked economic devastation on the economy. In 1873, the city appointed George A. Clough as the first city architect of Boston. Clough oversaw the rebuilding of the "burnt district," with high-rise office buildings and commercial blocks. By the turn of the 20th century, Downtown Boston had become an important banking and financial center in the United States, and the often elaborate and architecturally impressive buildings reflected that importance.

As the great John Ruskin once said, "True taste is forever growing, learning, reading, worshipping, laying its hand upon its mouth because it is astonished, lamenting over itself, and testing itself by the way it fits things." Maybe the readers of this book will grow in their appreciation of the history of Downtown Boston, learn of its changes since the advent of photography that recorded its evolution, and lay their hands over their mouths in astonishment at what has changed in the city, but realize, equally astonished, how much has really remained the same.

In the early 20th century, the Massachusetts State House had an impressive addition built to the rear of the original Bulfinch building of 1795, which was also on the site of the original Beacon Hill. Designed by noted architects Charles E. Brigham and John C. Spofford of Brigham & Spofford, it was completed in 1893 and greatly expanded the office space by sixfold. The extension was built of glazed yellow brick and limestone to match the original building, which was then painted yellow. The space constraints at the state house had been addressed in 1853, with an addition designed by Gridley J. Fox Bryant, and in 1867, when William Washburn made interior changes, but not until Brigham & Spofford's extension was built did the overcrowded conditions become alleviated. In the foreground is a sweeping drive that was obliterated when the white marble wings were added in 1917, designed by Chapman, Sturgis, and Andrews. To the left is an equestrian statue of Maj. Gen. Joseph Hooker, the famous Civil War hero.

Summer Street, laid out in 1683 and originally known as Mylne Street, was a fashionable residential neighborhood in the decades following the American Revolution. Known as the South End until the 1830s, when the present neighborhood of that name was being developed on filled land, it had impressive brick mansions with lavishly planted and well-tended gardens. This print, a view looking from Church Green at the corner of Bedford Street, shows the new South Church at the junction and Summer Street lined with lush shade trees that created a charming area of the city. Today, the area is completely commercial, with Devonshire Street on the right and large office buildings replacing the elegant mansions.

Chapter 1

THE OLD SOUTH END: DOWNTOWN CROSSING

The Vassall-Gardner House was a large colonial mansion set in a garden bounded by Summer, Washington, and Chauncy Streets. Built in 1727, the house and its impressive carriage house would survive until the years just prior to the Civil War as a rare example of the houses of Boston's Colonial elite. The mansion was demolished in 1854 by

George Gardner, who built a commercial block that was to become the site of C.F. Hovey's Store, known as importers, jobbers, and dry goods retailers, and which occupied the site from 1855 to 1949. The site was to later be that of Jordan Marsh Company (now Macy's), which was built in 1949 along Summer Street extending to Chauncy Street. The building was comprised of two city blocks and had a large addition designed by the noted architectural firm of Perry, Shaw & Hepburn. Here, the Summer Street façade has been pared down from its Colonial Revival design with a modernistic awning shading the large storefront display windows. The cast-iron fence in the foreground belongs to Trinity Church on Summer Street, and the crenelated tower in the distance was that of the Church of the Savior, organized in 1845. The Church of the Savior was designed by J.H. Hammatt Billings (1818–1874) and built on Bedford Street.

The Tontine Crescent was designed by Charles Bulfinch (1763–1848) and was considered a study in elegance and proportion, especially as Bulfinch was not a trained architect, but a "gentleman's architect." The second floor of the pavilion, with its modified Palladian window, was the first location of the Boston Library Society, founded in 1794. The third floor was used by the Massachusetts Historical Society (founded in 1791) from 1794 to 1833. As a convenient byway from Franklin to Summer Streets, an archway was designed in the pavilion, and that passageway has ever since been known as Arch Street. The elliptical green in the foreground had a large classical urn, which had been brought from England by Bulfinch and placed opposite the pavilion in memory of Benjamin Franklin, for whom the street was named. After 1858, the urn was set on the Bulfinch family lot at Mount Auburn Cemetery in Cambridge. Today, Arch Street is dominated by St. Anthony's Shrine, with was designed by the Franciscan Brother

Cajetan J.B. Baumann and built in 1955 with a monumental larger-than-life crucifix dominating the façade. Standing at the corner of Summer and Chauncy Streets and facing Arch Street, is the former Boston Five Cent Savings Bank, now a CVS Pharmacy with offices located above.

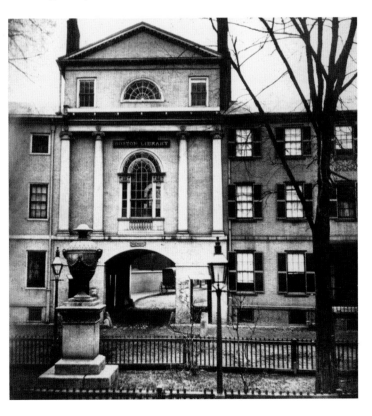

served a primarily French and Irish congregation. The cathedral was used as a place of worship until 1860, when the increasingly commercial aspect of the downtown caused the archdiocese to sell the land to Isaac Rich and purchase land on Washington Street in Boston's South End. The noted architect Patrick J. Keeley designed the new Cathedral of the Holy Cross on Washington Street in the South End. It was dedicated in 1875. On the right can be seen a corner of the Tontine Crescent and on the left, the spire of the Bulfinch-designed Federal Street Church, which was built in 1809. Today, the site is occupied by the modern Fleet Bank building, designed by Campbell, Aldrich, and Nulty and built in 1971. The Art Deco office building at Franklin and Devonshire Streets, adjacent to the Fleet Bank building, was designed by Parker, Thomas & Rice. Notice the fantastic light fixture on the left, which is in front of the former Boston Safe Deposit and Trust Company, now the Boston Stock Exchange, on Franklin Street.

The Church of the Holy Cross, designed by Charles Bulfinch, was built in 1803 at the east end of the Tontine Crescent for the Roman Catholics of Boston. The first Catholic Bishop in Boston was Jean-Louis A.M. LeFebvre de Cheverus (1768–1836). It was his engaging personality and simple piety that was to win over non Catholics who contributed to the building fund. With a simple, yet elegant, design, the building utilized the neoclassical design of the Tontine Crescent with Doric pilasters and a four-sided belfry. The church was later elevated to that of a cathedral, which

The Boston Theatre was designed by Charles Bulfinch and built in 1794 at the corner of Federal and Franklin Streets. Often referred to as the Old Drury, in hopeful comparison to Drury Lane in London, this was the first legitimate theatre in Boston. A brick building said to be "probably the most imposing theatre in the United States" at the time, it had an arcaded façade with Corinthian columns and pilasters that led to the foyer and two rows of boxes on the second floor. The pit and gallery were accessible by side doors. Elegant and spacious, the theatre also housed a ballroom and several retiring rooms for theatre patrons. In the late 18th century, many Bostonians still perceived the theatre as the Devil's workshop and believed that the frivolous plays performed there would cast all to Hell. When the theatre was destroyed by fire in 1798, the naysayers felt it was divine retribution. However, the theatre was quickly rebuilt with a new design by Charles Bulfinch, after which it became known as the Odeon Theatre.

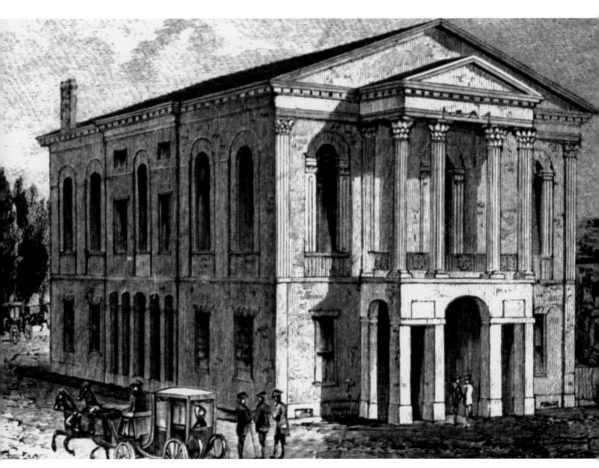

This elegant three-story federal house was designed by Charles Bulfinch and built in 1798 at the corner of Summer and Arch Streets. The house was built for John Tappan, a wealthy merchant and one of the many Bostonians to patronize Bulfinch as the architect of his new house. This elegant mansion was similar to the first Harrison Gray Otis house, designed by Bulfinch and built in 1796 in Boston's West End. Today, the Otis House is the headquarters of the Society for the Preservation of New England Antiquities (SPNEA), while the site of the Tappan House at the corner of Summer and Arch Streets is a blank-walled vacant commercial block that is currently awaiting a new tenant.

The duplex houses of the Welles and Gray families were built *c.* 1812 at the corner of Summer and Kingston Streets in the fashionable neighborhood of the old South End. The houses shared a uniform height with swell bay façades on either corner, and the entrances had paired columns supporting a lintel, which was surmounted by a cast-iron balcony. On the site of these houses, Leman Klous built the hoop skirt manufacturing store and warehouse in which the Great Boston Fire started on November 9, 1872. The present building dates to 1873 and is a four-story commercial structure with a dormer mansard roof. The first floor houses Salon Picasso and Kingston Deli.

The New South Church, or the Octagonal Church, as it was often referred to, was designed by Charles Bulfinch and built in 1814 at the junction of Bedford and Summer Streets. The New South Church was an impressive addition to the fashionable old South End of Boston. It faced a cast-iron fence enclosing a well-tended green, which gave its name to what henceforth was to become known as Church Green. As the neighborhood of the old South End changed from a residential to a commercial one, the Octagonal Church was closed and later demolished in 1868. The present building, known as the Church Green Building, was built after the Great Boston Fire of 1872 and used by the Read Shoe Company (later Read & White), as it was located in the shoe and leather district of Boston. Today, a high-rise stepped office building looms high above the original mansard-roofed structure. On the left are the street façades of the post–1873 buildings, with 125 Summer Street, designed by Kohn, Pederson, and Fox and built in 1990, rising above the buildings.

C hurch Green, looking towards Summer Street from Bedford Street, had the impressive Doric colonnade and bracketed pediment of the New South Church on the left and the fashionable mansions at the corner of Winthrop Place. The two row houses in the distance originally belonged to Henry Gassett and William Sturgis, after which they gave way to the Simmons Block. Today, this is the site of 100 Summer Street, located at the corner of Devonshire Street. In the distance rises the Fleet Bank building, which was designed by Campbell, Aldrich & Nulty and built in 1971.

Chauncey Street, which extends from Essex to Summer Streets, was the site of the third edifice of the First Church of Boston, which was designed by Asher Benjamin and built in 1808. The First Church had been founded in 1632

and was initially on King (now State) Street, after which a new church was built at the corner of Washington and Court Streets. The congregation worshiped here until 1868, when a new church designed by Ware & Van Brundt was built in Boston's Back Bay. To the left of the church was the Chauncey Hall School, a preparatory school located here until the 1870s, when it moved to Copley Square in Boston's Back Bay. The mansard-roofed building is the Italian Renaissance-style Massachusetts Charitable Mechanic Association, designed by J.H. Hammatt Billings (1818–1874) and built in 1860. Today, the rear of Macy's extension, designed by Perry, Shaw & Hebburn, faces Chauncy Street with the utilitarian addition of the Suissotel to its left. On the right is the 1873 building of the former Long's Jewelry Store, now Citizens Bank, at 40 Summer Street.

Trinity Church, organized in 1733 and the oldest Episcopalian parish in the city, was designed by George Brimmer and built in 1829 at the corner of Summer and Hawley Streets (formerly known as Bishop's Alley). A substantial and solid church, it was built of massive rough-hewn granite blocks "in a solid Gothic [style] and intended to reproduce the old English type of the Episcopal temple with a squat crenelated tower." On the left is Thorndike Hall, which stood on Summer Street near Washington Street and the present site of Filene's department store. Washington Street can be seen in the distance. The Masonic bodies in Boston met in Thorndike Hall after the Masonic Temple on Tremont Street was destroyed by fire in 1866. By 1870, the site was that of George Hill & Company, after which it became that of Filene's department store, opened by Edward

Filene. On the far right is a corner of the former Kennedy's department store—its 1873 cast-iron façade was saved in the early 1980s and incorporated into a new high-rise office building at 101 Arch Street. On the left is the former Gilchrist department store.

Franklin Street, once a fashionable residential area, was swept away in 1858 and four-story granite commercial buildings, designed by Gridley J. Fox Bryant, were built on the site of Bulfinch's Tontine Crescent. Interestingly, the new buildings utilized the same gently sweeping curve of the street and shared a uniformity of roof levels and building materials. The last remnant of the once lush green is a sole surviving shade tree, which has been ringed with a protective embankment. Today, Bulfinch's design of a gently curving sweep of Franklin Street survives. This photograph shows the Wigglesworth Building on the left, designed by Nathaniel J. Bradlee and William T. Winslow and dating from 1873. The Boston Stock Exchange building, formerly the Boston Safe Deposit & Trust Company, is seen on the right. (Courtesy William Varrell.)

On the occasion of the 50th anniversary of the opening of Quincy Market, the festivities were augmented by Brown's Brigade Band, whose members are lined up in regimental fashion, as well as stallholders, who paraded with great éclat. A large crowd stands on either side of the South Market as the brass band pauses for a photograph. Alexander Parris's design for Quincy Market was obvious in this photograph due to the use of Quincy granite for a domed pavilion with flanking wings on either side that had Doric-columned porticos. Ames Plow Company had numerous signs on the market, as did other businesses located here. On the right is a corner of a granite warehouse designed by Gridley J. Fox Bryant and built in 1852. This warehouse is now the site of Marketplace Center, which was designed by the architectural firm of WZMH Group and built in 1985. In the distance, Faneuil Hall can be seen with its copper grasshopper weathervane made by Dea. Shem Drowne in 1742. Faneuil Hall is often referred to as Boston's "cradle of liberty," and it had to be

Chapter 2

THE HAYMARKET: QUINCY MARKET

enlarged to its present proportions in 1806 by Charles Bulfinch. Beyond the hall can be seen the area of Brattle Street, which is now the site of Boston City Hall and its plaza. (Courtesy Boston Athenaeum.)

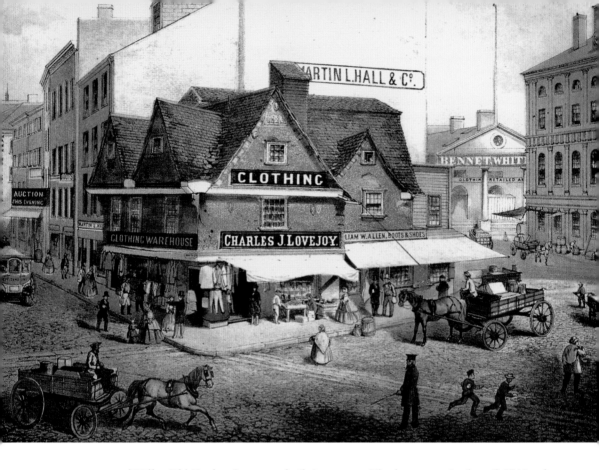

The Old Feather Store was built in 1680 on the edge of North Street and Dock Square, which is the area of the Haymarket. This stucco-covered wood house, built by Thomas Staniford, was an important example of a 17th-century house with an overhang.

The house survived until 1860, when it was demolished. By 1820, the Old Feather Store, once a fashionable 17th-century residence with a multitude of gables, became the store of John K. Simpson Jr. Simpson sold feathers, mattresses, and bed ticking. Later, in the mid-19th century, Charles J. Lovejoy operated a clothing warehouse in the building. In the distance, the pedimented colonnade of Quincy Market with a large sign advertising Bennet, White & Company clothiers is shown. On the far left is a horse-drawn omnibus of the Citizens Line, which connected all parts of the city. Today, the site has become the greenhouses of Exotic Flowers, designed by Benjamin Thompson Associates, which create an interesting modernistic juxtaposition of sloping glass roofs to the older buildings along North Street. On the right can be seen Faneuil Hall with the tower of the Boston Custom House rising above it.

Built in 1742 from designs provided by the noted Scottish artist John Smibert, Faneuil Hall was the gift to the town of Boston from Peter Faneuil, Esq. (1700–1743), a wealthy Huguenot merchant. The hall's deed states that it must always have a place of business on its first floor. It was greatly enlarged in 1805 by noted architect Charles Bulfinch (1763–1848) when it was doubled in size and a third floor was added. Here, in Faneuil Hall Square—the space between the hall and Quincy Market—the east façade of Faneuil Hall has arched windows with pilasters between them and an octagonal cupola. From the time the hall was built in 1742, all town meetings were held in the second-floor hall, as well as public demonstrations, receptions for distinguished guests and visitors to Boston, banquets, and balls. The third floor has been occupied by the armory of the Ancient and Honorable Artillery Company, where they have maintained a museum for many years. Today, the area has become a destination spot, not just for tourists, but also for native Bostonians due to the numerous street shows and musicians entertaining the crowds.

Throughout the 19th century, the Haymarket of Boston contained the area of Faneuil Hall and Quincy Market. The overcrowded and unsanitary conditions of the Faneuil Hall Marketplace led to the infilling of the Dock Square area, with a new market and two warehouses flanking it, as well as the creation of six new streets.

Large numbers of horse-drawn wagons and delivery carts throng South Market in this late-19th-century photograph. The infilling plan, which was to be financed by the taxpayers of the new city of Boston, was strongly opposed by those taxpayers. However, the second mayor of the city, Josiah Quincy (1772–1864), pressed forward, and with architect Alexander Parris (1780–1852), created not just an imposing market, but a sanitary marketplace with ample supplies of produce, meats, and provisions, which were replenished daily. Today, looking through the shade trees planted in the late 1970s, the area known as Faneuil Hall Square is packed with people throughout the day and evening hours. As J.F. Cooper said in *Lionel Lincoln,* "The patriotism of the meetings in 'Old Funnel' rang from the North End to the Neck."

A c. 1870 view looking down South Market Street from Faneuil Hall towards Quincy Market shows a large number of vendors trading their goods. Quincy Market was named for Josiah Quincy (1772–1864), the second mayor of the city of Boston, who served from 1823 to 1828 and "invested the sluggish town with new life, and brought into practical use a new watchword, 'progress.'" The market was 535-feet long, with a central pavilion that rises 87 feet and was surmounted by a dome. The market stalls occupied the first floor, with warerooms above. The large hall under the dome, known as Quincy Hall, was the meeting room of the Boston Chamber of Commerce. The halls were often used for exhibitions and fairs of groups, including the New England Society for the Promotion of Manufactures and the Mechanic Arts. The south side of Faneuil

Hall has changed relatively little in the last century, and a kiosk of Bostix, a purveyor of tickets, can be seen on the right. (Courtesy William Varrell.)

Depicted in a *c.*1835 print by the artist and architect J.H. Hammatt Billings, a group of canvas-covered wagons wait on the side of South Market Street to unload their produce at Quincy Market. With daily provisions brought to the market, often by boat before the light of dawn, the supplies were quoted to be the "best produce of the fields...and slaughter houses of our vicinity." Quincy Market was said at the time of its completion to be "among the most commodious, conveniently arranged, and best-equipped market-houses in the country," and was actually Boston's second supermarket—the first being Boylston Market, which was opened in 1809 at the corner of Washington and Boylston Streets. By 1826, this market was opened near the old Haymarket where town residents could shop for goods. The Massachusetts Horticultural Society was established in 1829, with its early meetings being held in the office of the Russell Seed Store at 52 North Market Street. The first of the horticultural society's exhibitions was held in Quincy Hall, the second floor of the granite market.

The Doric-columned arcade of
Quincy Market had stalls with
displays on either side of a center aisle.
The stall on the right is that of Davis,
Chapin & Company, with a display of
canned vegetables in front of a colonnade
of Doric columns. The stallkeepers
furnished daily supplies of provisions to
both city and suburban homes, as well
as to wholesale provision dealers, in a
sanitary environment, as envisioned by
Mayor Josiah Quincy. Today, though
the stalls are occupied by fast-food
purveyors and specialty shops, the market
owes a great debt to the man whose
plans for the infilling of the town dock
anticipated a marketplace. Since Quincy
Market opened in 1978, after having
been revamped by James Rouse of the
Rouse Corporation and noted architect
Benjamin Thompson, the former stalls
have been thronged with tourists and
shoppers. (Courtesy William Varrell.)

North Market, on the right, flanked Quincy Market with a row of commercial buildings that shared a uniform roof cornice and granite façade. Notice the repetitive dormers along the slate roofs that create an interesting pattern along the row. The famous Durgin Park Restaurant and Cottrell's Dining Room can be seen on the right, with numerous horse-drawn delivery wagons unloading their goods in the foreground. Today, office workers on their lunch hour and tourists throng the North and South Markets. In the distance can be seen Boston City Hall, which was designed by Kallmann, McKinnell & Knowles. It was built in 1967 as the center of a vast plaza designed by I.M. Pei and carved out of the former Scollay, Adams, and Winthrop Square areas of Boston.

The Boston Custom House, seen in an 1850 stereo view, was designed by Ammi Burnham Young, assisted by J.H. Hammatt Billings, and was built between 1837 and 1849 at the head of Long Wharf. The earlier customhouse had been built in 1810 on Custom House Street, but it was moved closer to the waterfront when this impressive Greek cross granite building was completed in 1849. The newer building had 32 massive Doric columns of Quincy granite encircling the building, all of which supported the cornice, and a center dome that was 25 feet in diameter and sheathed with wrought granite tiles. Each of these columns weighed 42 tons, was brought from the granite dressing sheds in East Milton by teams of oxen, and required more than 3,000 wood pilings to be driven into the ground to support their great weight.

In 1890, the Boston Custom House was photographed from the corner of State and India Streets with the circular, pinnacled façade of the Boston Chamber of Commerce rising above it in the distance. By this time, the waterfront had been infilled and no longer did Boston Harbor come up to the building. Eventually, the federal government commissioned Peabody & Stearns to build the tower above the Boston Custom House. As a result, the interior rotunda was removed, with eight of the twelve Corinthian columns originally supporting the dome being taken to Franklin Park, where they were used in creating an archway entrance to the grounds, recently landscaped by Frederick Law Olmstead and the Olmstead Associates.

The Boston Chamber of Commerce
was organized in 1885 with the
merger of the Commercial and Produce
Exchanges, the object being "to promote
just and equitable principles of trade,
to establish and maintain uniformity
in commercial usages, to correct any
abuses which may exist, to acquire,
preserve, and disseminate valuable
business information... and generally,
to advance the interests of trade and
commerce in the city of Boston." The
Chamber of Commerce (now referred
to as the Grain and Flower Exchange)
building was designed by Shepley, Rutan
& Coolidge and built of rough-hewn
pink Worcester granite at the junction of
India Street and Central Wharf in 1892.
An impressive modified Gothic building
with pinnacled crenelation surrounding
a turreted roof, the building had trade

rooms, reading rooms, committee rooms,
and offices. Today, the crenelated building
is dwarfed by the twin Harbor Tower
Condominiums that rise on the edge of
Boston Harbor, designed by Henry Cobb
of I.M. Pei & Partners.

31

Downtown Boston was never more impressive or imposing than it is in this 1916 photograph, which shows the recently completed Boston Custom House tower, designed by the noted Boston architectural firm of Peabody & Stearns and built in 1915 above the original Greek Revival structure that had been completed in 1849. The Boston Custom House was an important federal building located just south of State Street and is today the Marriott Custom House. On the left can be seen the Boston Board of Trade building, and on the right is the Boston Chamber of Commerce, said in the early 20th century to be one of the "most aggressive commercial bodies in any American city."

Tremont Street, at the intersection of Park and Winter Streets, was at a virtual standstill when this photograph was taken in 1930. Tremont is a corruption of "Trimount," a word that paid homage to the three hills of Boston—Mount Vernon, Beacon and Pemberton Hills. The street was one of the original streets of the 17th century and ran along the east edge of the Boston Common. On the left of this photograph is the Park Street Church, known as "Brimstone Corner," not necessarily due to the storage of gunpowder in its basement during the War of 1812 as much as for its fiery abolitionist, orthodox doctrines and anti-slavery orations, among which many were given by William Lloyd Garrison, who edited the weekly newspaper *The Liberator* from 1831 to 1863.

Chapter 3

TRIMOUNT: TREMONT STREET

King's Chapel was organized in 1686, with its first place of worship being built in 1689. The present church of granite blocks was built on the site of the first chapel at the corner of Tremont and School Streets and was designed by Peter Harrison, who was considered to be the first architect in Boston. The King's Chapel burial ground adjacent to the chapel was the first place of burial in Boston after 1630, with such luminaries as Govs. John Winthrop and William Shirley, Rev. John Cotton, Capt. Roger Clap, and Hester Prynne, the infamous bearer of the scarlet letter, as immortalized by Nathaniel Hawthorne. Following the American Revolution, the church was often referred to as the Stone Chapel in abhorrence of anything to do with British rule or England. It was here in 1787 that the Rev. James Freeman became pastor, under whose influence the church embraced Unitarianism, the first church in this country to do so. Here, a horse-drawn barouche stops in front of the Ionic-columned portico that was added by Charles Bulfinch in 1789 for George Washington's impending visit to Boston. Rising just above the roof of the church can be seen the dome of Boston's old city hall. King's Chapel is today dwarfed by the numerous high-rise office buildings of Downtown Boston. (Courtesy William Varrell.)

By the 1840s, Tremont Street had become an impressive thoroughfare, with not just King's Chapel, seen in the center, but the Greek Revival Tremont House, on the left, and the neoclassical Tremont Theatre, on the right. The Tremont House was designed by Isaiah Rogers and opened to the public as the first luxury hotel in 1829. The Tremont Theatre, known as the Tremont Temple after 1843, when it was purchased by the Union Temple Baptist Church, was designed by Isaiah Rogers and built in 1827 as a "theatre of high standard."

Looking down Hamilton Place toward Tremont Street in 1885, this view of the dead-end street allows for the façade and spire of the Park Street Church to be seen in its full splendor. The first public signing of "America" took place at the Park Street Church, and its members were a prominent part of the abolitionist movement prior to the Civil War. Once a fashionable residential street, it is today the entrance to the former Boston Music Hall, which was designed by George Snell and also served as the place of worship for Theodore Parker's 28th Congregational Society. It is now the Orpheum Theatre, which has a large arched entrance at the dead end of Hamilton Place. The David J. Sargeant Hall, built in 1999 as the new Suffolk University Law School, is on the left side of the place. Henry James said of Hamilton Place in his book *The Bostonians* that as "he gazed down the vista, the approach for pedestrians...he thought it looked expectant and ominous."

Looking down Tremont Street from Bromfield Street, the spire of the Park Street Church dominates the streetscape. On the right can be seen the Old Granary Burial Ground and its granite Egyptian Revival gateway that was designed by noted architect Isaiah Rogers. Rogers used Quincy granite for its corner piers and had three-dimensional hourglass motifs carved into the granite, signifying the passing of time. Along Tremont Street, huge slabs of granite were placed with a cast-iron fence surmounting the street. The Old Granary Burial Ground, laid out in 1660 adjacent to the town granary at the corner of Park Street, was the final resting place of such luminaries as Elizabeth Vergoose, also known as "Mother Goose;" benefactor Peter Faneuil; Govs. Richard Bellingham, William Dummer, James Bowdoin, John Hancock, Samuel Adams, James Sullivan, Christopher Gore, William Eustis, and Increase Sumner; first mayor of Boston John Phillips; patriot and silversmith Paul Revere; and the five victims of the Boston Massacre of 1770, Samuel Gray, Samuel Maverick, James Caldwell, Crispus Attucks, and Patrick Carr. On the left can be seen the swell bay façade of the David J. Sargeant Hall of the Suffolk Law School.

The Tremont House was the first luxury hotel in the city. It was designed by Isaiah Rogers and built in 1829 with a façade of Quincy granite and an impressive portico of four bold Doric columns. The Tremont House, which had been built for Messrs. Elliot, Belknap, and Upham, was once described as having "always been a first-class hotel, and has had a reputation for solid comfort and quiet elegance in its conduct....[and the] efficient management of the house early attained a national reputation." Many notable guests stayed at the Tremont House, but it was the English author Charles Dickens who described the hotel during his stay as having "more galleries, colonnades, piazzas, and passages than I can remember, or the reader would believe." On the lower left of the photograph can be seen a portion of the Egyptian gateway and cast-iron fence in front of the Old Granary Burial Ground. On the far right is George W. Safford & Company, a shop that offered perfumery, toilet articles, and soap. The Tremont Building at 73 Tremont Street was designed by the Boston architectural firm of Winslow & Wetherall and built in 1895 on the site of the old hotel. The first tenant of the new building was S.S. Pierce & Company, whose president was Wallace Lincoln Pierce (1852–1920). The firm leased the ground-floor store at the corner of Tremont and Beacon Streets, across the street from its first store at the corner of Tremont and Court Streets. The building at 73 Tremont Street underwent a renovation by Childs, Bertman, Tseckares in 1990.

Looking down Tremont Street from Park Street, the steps of the Park Street Church can be seen on the right. On the left are buildings with a wide range of architectural styles, from Hamilton Place to West Street. The red brick neoclassical building on the corner tries to replicate the light tracery and elegant proportions of Bullfinch's designs, while the remainder of the streetscape goes the gamut of late-19th-century commercial blocks to those of the early 20th century. This segment of Tremont Street, opposite the Park Street Church and facing the Massachusetts State House, deserves a more cohesive and unifying architectural theme rather than the assemblage of present buildings.

St. Paul's Church was designed by Alexander Parris (1780–1852) and built in 1820. The church was built of gray granite, with massive Ionic columns, carved by Solomon Willard, of Potomac sandstone. Consecrated by the Episcopal bishops of Massachusetts and Connecticut, the congregation envisioned an important and influential church. The pediment had blocks of sandstone that were intended to be carved, but for a lack of funds they were never executed and remain as such to this day. The first rector of St. Paul's Church was Rev. Samuel F. Jarvis, who served from 1820 to 1825. A coachman pulls up in front of the church in 1895. According to the church sign to the right of the front entrance, there was a "Litany Today." Since 1908, St. Paul's Church has served as the cathedral of the Diocese of Massachusetts and has a busy outreach program in addition to Sunday services. On the right is the former R.H. Stearns department store, designed by the Boston architectural firm of Parker, Thomas & Rice. Today, it is senior housing.

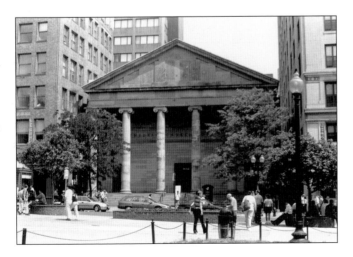

Looking down Park Street from the Massachusetts State House, the Amory-Ticknor House can be seen on the left with the former Abbott Lawrence House, now the Union Club of Boston, to its right. Along Park Street were row houses designed by Charles Bulfinch and built in 1808. The spire of the Park Street Church rises high above the area, and an allee of shade trees along the edge of the Boston Common can be seen on the right. The Amory-Ticknor House was remodeled *c.* 1895 with two-story Queen Anne-inspired oriel windows of black-painted pressed metal and fanciful dormers on the Park Street roofline. Surprisingly, the graceful entrance, with its paired fluted columns, survived, but is now flanked with first-floor shops.

The Masonic Temple was designed by Richard Bond and built in 1831 of triangular pieces of granite quarried in Quincy. It was the first building of the Masonic Fraternity in Boston. It was sold to the federal government in 1858 for use as a courthouse. In 1885, it was sold by the federal government, two stories were added, and the building was completely remodeled for business purposes. An imposing twin-towered granite building with pinnacles on the four corners of the towers, it stood at the corner of Tremont Street and Temple Place. On the left of the photograph can be seen the façade of St. Paul's Church. Today, the former R.H. Stearns department store, which was designed by the Boston architectural firm of Parker, Thomas & Rice, is on the temple's former site. It houses stores on the first floor, while the upper floors have been converted to senior residences, which have superb views of the Boston Common and the setting sun in the west.

Looking along Tremont Street in 1870, Gleason's Publishing Hall is on the right between Bromfield and Bosworth Streets. The impressive building with a colonnade of Corinthian columns was built in 1841 for the Boston Museum, a theatre operated by Moses Kimball. In the mid-19th century, theatres were often referred to as "museums" to lessen the stigma of ladies attending theatrical performances. Frederick Gleason was the publisher of *Gleason's Pictorial Drawing Room Companion,* a weekly illustrated newspaper that was published here until the building was demolished in 1865. On the far left can be seen the portico of King's Chapel, the façade of the Parker House Hotel, and the Tremont Temple, which was replaced by a grand Italianate design building, designed by Clarence H. Blackall and built in 1896. The new hotel and restaurant Nine Zero is next to the Paddock Building, designed by John A. Fox (1835–1920) and built in 1910 at 101 Tremont Street. The Paddock Building was named for the Paddock Elms that

once graced the sidewalk in front of the Old Granary Burial Ground. Suffolk University recently built the impressive Suffolk University Law School, known as David J. Sargeant Hall, seen on the right.

In 1864, the Massachusetts Horticultural Society commissioned noted Boston architect Gridley J. Fox Bryant to design its second headquarters, which would be located on Tremont Street, between Bromfield Street and Montgomery Place, and opposite the Granary Burial Ground. An impressive building of Concord white granite with copious details such as Doric columns on the first floor, Ionic columns on the second floor, and Corinthian columns on the third floor, the headquarters held a life-sized statue of Cerces surmounting the parapet, while smaller statues of Flora and Pomona flanked the corners, all of which were sculpted by the noted sculptor Martin Milmore.

King's Chapel, the Parker House, and Tremont Temple create an eclectic architectural streetscape in this 1890 photograph. The Parker House, which was opened by Harvey D. Parker (1804–1884) in 1855 in the former Horticultural Hall on School Street, was to become one of Boston's most prominent late-19th-century hotels. It would also become world famous as the originator of the Parker House Roll and Boston Cream Pie. The original hotel was designed by William Washburn, and was built of marble with a graceful chateau roof and oriel windows on the corners of the building. The hotel was further expanded in 1886 with Gridley J. Fox Bryant building an extension for Joseph Beckman and Edward Punchard, former partners of Parker. Built in 1853 on the site of the old Tremont Theatre, the Tremont Temple was the place of worship for the Union Temple Church and the

New England headquarters of the Baptist Church. The present Tremont Temple, with an Italianate façade of tapestry brick and classical architectural details, was designed by Clarence H. Blackall and built in 1895.

45

Seen here in 1928, relatively little has changed in this view of Tremont Street in the last few decades. The Park Street Church was designed by the English architect Peter Banner and was built in 1809 of red brick with a graceful spire, the capitals of which were carved by Solomon Willard. An active church in missionary work throughout the world, the Park Street Church has seen numerous churches that were established due to its aggressive outreach. The church was built on the site of the old granary, a gristmill that was moved to Commercial Point in Dorchester and refitted as a sail making concern. The granary gave its name to the burial ground adjacent to it, which was once a part of the Boston Common and was used as early as 1660 as a place of burial. The large granite Egyptian gateway was designed by Isaiah Rogers and erected in 1840, along with the cast-iron fence along Tremont Street. In the distance can be seen the Tremont Building, which was designed by the architectural firm of Winslow & Wetherall and built in 1895 on the site of the old Tremont House. On the far left is a part of the kiosk to the subway at Park Street Station, which was designed by Edmund March Wheelwright, Boston city architect, and built in 1905.

The Massachusetts State House rises high on Beacon Hill as seen from the corner of Tremont and Park Streets in this *c.* 1905 photograph. Designed by Charles Bulfinch, the cornerstone was laid in 1795 by Gov. Samuel Adams (1722–1803). The Masonic service was performed by the Most Worshipful Paul Revere, grand master of the Union Lodge of Masons. Having been built on the slope of Beacon Hill, the Massachusetts State House is a prominent landmark in Boston and rises high above Boston Common. The neoclassical red brick building has an impressive colonnade of Corinthian columns and a dome that was covered in gold leaf in 1874. The building was restored in 1896 by Arthur Everett of the Boston architectural firm of Cabot, Everett & Mead. On the right can be seen the corner of the Park Street Church, and on the left is seen a portion of the Boston Common.

Chapter 4

AROUND SENTRY HILL: WEST END

The Hancock House was built of granite in 1737 on Beacon Street, which was then considered somewhat removed from town, and was among the most elegant and commodious of 18th-century houses in Boston. The home of Thomas Hancock (1703–1764) and

Lydia Henchman Hancock (1714–1777), it was later inherited by their nephew and heir, the great patriot John Hancock (1737–1793). Though there was a move to preserve the house as a possible residence for the governor of Massachusetts, the house was ignobly razed in 1863. A duplex French Second Empire house for the Brewer and Beebe families was built on the site of the patriot's home, which survived until 1917 when the Massachusetts State House was expanded and white marble wings were added. On a portion of the Hancock garden was built the Unitarian Universalist Association building in 1925, which was a revival house designed by Eliot T. Putnam. The Boston architectural firm of Putnam & Cox worked to replicate those early-19th-century townhouses at the corner of Beacon and Joy Streets.

The Massachusetts State House, seen in 1892, was designed by Charles Bulfinch and built in 1798 on the slope of Beacon Hill. Its pineapple surmounted lantern, which caps the gold-leafed dome, is 220 feet above sea level. In front of the state house are bronze statues of the great statesman Daniel Webster, sculpted by Hiram Powers, and on the left is the great educator Horace Mann, sculpted by Emma Stebbins. The grounds also include a seated statue of the Quaker martyr Mary Dyer and of John Fitzgerald Kennedy (1917–1963.) As Holmes once said, the "Boston State House is the Hub of the Solar System. You couldn't pry that out of a Boston man if you had the tire of all creation straightened out for a crowbar." The gold-leafed dome of the state house was once the tallest in Boston, and on a sunny day the sun's reflection glints and attracts one's attention through

the multitude of high-rise buildings. On the right can be seen the flagpoles that project from the façade of the Union Club of Boston.

Pemberton Square was an elegant square laid out in 1835 on the remains of the once 75-foot high Pemberton (formerly Cotton) Hill, which, like Beacon Hill, had been leveled for developer Patrick T. Jackson. Accessed from Tremont Street via Court (formerly known as Queen) and Somerset Streets, the square was developed from the former

estate and terraced gardens of Gardiner Greene. On the right, bow-fronted row houses face a tree-lined green that is enclosed with a cast-iron fence, and flat-façaded row houses are on the left. The square, like its famous counterpart, Louisburg Square, attracted prominent Boston families, among them members of the Sigorney, Winthrop, Bowdoin, Lowell, Brooks, Forbes, and Shattuck families. By the 1880s, the once pleasant square was located adjacent to Scollay Square, a bustling and noisy crossroads, and most of the families had departed. The area was chosen to build the new Suffolk County Courthouse, which was designed by George A. Clough, Boston city architect, and built in 1896. Today, the Suffolk County Courthouse dominates the western side of the plaza. The rear of 1, 2, and 3 Center Plaza, designed by Welton Beckett and Associates, creates a modern crescent-shaped façade that screens the plaza of Boston City Hall.

The Scollay Building was built in 1795 at the intersection of Court and Tremont Streets. Below, in an 1865 photograph, the building has numerous signs advertising auction rooms, a farm agency, advertising agency, and the ticket office of the Middlesex Railroad Station. The building was purchased in 1800 by William Scollay, a successful apothecary whose shop was on Cornhill. It was for him that the square in front of the building was named. The Scollay Building was razed in 1871. This area was also the site of 109 Court Street, which was, in 1875, the site of the first sound transmitted over wires. Alexander Graham Bell and Thomas A. Watson were the pioneers of sound that led to the birthplace of the telephone—something we take for granted today. A recent addition to the area is a steel-and-wood pergola, which has modernistic seating overlooking the plaza.

Scollay Square was the junction of Tremont and Court Streets and Cornhill and Tremont Row. In this photograph, the square has a horse-drawn omnibus passing through the intersection with Pemberton Square seen in the distance. The square once had a bronze statue of Gov. John Winthrop placed in its center in 1880. The statue is today in the garden of the First and Second Church in Boston, at the corner of Berkeley and Marlborough Streets in Boston's Back Bay. The copper-sheathed Gothic spire of the Somerset Street (after 1877 the First Free Will) Baptist Church on Somerset Street rises above the houses on the left, and a corner of the Scollay Building can be seen on the right. The area was redeveloped in the mid-1960s with Center Plaza, a curving building designed by Welton Becket & Associates, dominating the curve facing City Hall Plaza and creating a screen for the Suffolk County Courthouse.

The Suffolk County Courthouse was designed by George A. Clough and built in 1896 facing Pemberton Square. The massive building was later enlarged in 1936 by Desmond & Lord. On the right, a few of the row houses that once lined the square survive, no longer as residences, but as commercial buildings. Seen in the center, Barristers Hall was built in 1910 and demolished in 1965 to make way for Center Plaza, which is a sweeping crescent that was designed by Welton Becket & Associates.

By 1900, Pemberton Square had changed dramatically from the tree-shaded square of the mid-19th century to a densely built up street with the Suffolk County Courthouse on the left and office buildings on the right. The office buildings had a large number of attorneys' and court offices due to their proximity to the courthouse.

The Leopold Morse department store was built at the corner of Washington and Brattle Streets in the West End. The store was established in 1852 by Jacob Morse, Ferdinand Strauss, and Louis Strauss and was, at the turn of the 20th century, the oldest retail clothing house in Boston. The son of one of the founders of the store, Leopold Morse also served as a member of the United States House of Representatives and was a benefactor of the Morse Home for Aged and Infirm Hebrews and Orphanage, which was opened and operated in 1889 in Milton until 1914, when it was moved to Dorchester. Here, the department store is bedecked with bunting and flags for the nation's centennial in 1875. On the left can be seen a corner of the Lovell Building. (Courtesy Boston Athenaeum, Print Room.)

The Lovell Building was located in Adams Square, which was named for the patriot and governor Samuel Adams (1722–1803) and had a bronze statue sculpted by Anne Whitney. The Adams statue stands today on a granite plinth in front of Faneuil Hall facing Boston City Hall, and its stern visage is little deterrent for the multitude of pigeons that flock to it. John P. Lovell, proprietor of the store, was an importer and dealer in guns, rifles, pistols, and fishing tackle. In this photograph, a horse-drawn streetcar passes the statue of the great patriot Samuel Adams, who served not only in the Massachusetts Legislature, but was a delegate to the Continental Congress, when he originally overlooked the busy intersection. On the right is the Leopold Morse department store with its oriel clock tower. Today, the Washington Mall replaces the street with the pink granite base of 28 State Street, designed by Edward Larrabee Barnes and built in 1969 for the New England Merchants National Bank, and One Washington Mall, designed by Eduardo Catalano and built in 1969. In the distance can be seen the new high-rise known as the Residences of the Ritz Carlton Hotel being built near the Theatre District between Tremont and Washington Streets.

Scollay Square was a bustling area, as seen in this photograph from 1880. Numerous streetcars connecting all parts of the city travel along Court Street. The statue of Gov. John Winthrop (1588–1649), sculpted by Horatio Greenough, can be seen in the foreground, the area that was referred to as Winthrop Square. The infamous Crawford House with its awninged windows can be seen on the right center at the corner of Court and Brattle Streets. Though the Crawford House was known for its burlesque and striptease shows, the first floor of this Gothic Revival building was the site of the National Security Bank, founded in 1867. Therefore, patrons were using the building day and night. The once vibrant area was rebuilt in the 1960s with the new Boston City Hall, designed by Kallmann, McKinnell & Knowles. The city hall sits on a nine-acre brick paved plaza designed by I.M. Pei. The 26-story John Fitzgerald

Kennedy federal office building, designed by The Architects Collaborative (TAC) and Samuel Glaser Associates, was also rebuilt in the 1960s.

Scollay Square, seen in 1903, had an elaborate subway kiosk designed by Edmund March Wheelwright and erected in 1898 in the center of the square—the former site of the Scollay Building until it was razed in 1871. In the distance is the Hemenway Building, which was an office building designed by Nathaniel J. Bradlee and built of red brick and hewn brownstone in 1880 for the Augustus Hemenway Estate. To the left is the Scollay Building of the United States Trust Company. Today, on the far left, is the high-rise office building of Mellon Financial Center at One Boston Place, which was designed by Pietro Belluschi, and on the right is the curve of Center Plaza. The gold-leafed steaming kettle mounted above Starbucks Coffee on the far left reads that its capacity is 227 gallons, 2 quarts, 1 pint, and 3 gills. The teakettle looms at the edge of the Sears Block, which was built in 1848 and was restored by Frederick A. Stahl & Associates.

Washington Street, between Summer and Milk Streets, had impressive buildings built on it after the Great Boston Fire of 1872. On the right, at the corner of Franklin Street, are numerous small businesses with the imposing spire of the Old South Meeting House in the distance. The Old South Meeting House, officially the Third Church of Boston, had been organized in 1669. The present meetinghouse was designed by Joshua Blanchard and built in 1727. The scene of tumultuous meetings during the period between the Boston Massacre in 1770 and the evacuation of the British and Loyalists in 1776, the Old South Meeting House became an integral part of Boston until it was abandoned as a place of worship in 1872 when the congregation built the New Old South Church in Boston's Back Bay.

Chapter 5

WASHINGTON STREET: DOWNTOWN CROSSING

Oliver Wendell Holmes said of the Old Corner Bookstore in his *Over the Teacups,* "I never can go into that famous 'Corner Bookstore' and look over the new books...without seeing half a dozen which I want to read, or at least to know something about." The Old Corner Bookstore has been continuously occupied by a bookstore since 1828, when Timothy Carter remodeled the then century-old building as a bookshop. Built in 1712 by apothecary Thomas Crease at the corner of Washington and School Streets on the site of the house of Anne

Hutchinson, who was banished from the Massachusetts Bay Colony in 1634 in regard to her opposition of authority and religious beliefs, the bookstore has long been a landmark in the city. In the 19th century, it became famous as the location where *The North American Review,* the oldest magazine in the nation, and the *Atlantic Monthly* were published. It has been the bookstore of Carter & Hardee, as well as the book shop of such prominent firms as Ticknor & Fields, E.P. Dutton & Company, and that of Damrell & Upham. It is said to have become a favorite spot of Bostonians, "the writers and students of literature long were accustomed to gather in their daily interchange of good-fellowship and art, as if an inspiration were to be drawn from the quaint gables and odd staircases, and crannies which have looked down upon almost two centuries of life and progress." Saved in 1960 from an ignoble fate by Historic Boston, Inc., who took title to the building, the Globe Old Corner Bookstore, with its 1828 addition along School Street, represents one of the few 17th-century buildings to survive in Boston.

The Old South Meeting House was designed by Joshua Blanchard and built in 1729 at the corner of Washington and Milk Streets. The congregation had been organized in 1669 and was to worship here until 1876 when the New Old South Church was designed by Cummings & Sears and built at the corner of Boylston and Dartmouth Streets in Boston's Back Bay. During the tumultuous years of the American Revolution, Old South was the scene of fiery orations as well as from where the Mohawk Indians departed to participate in the Boston Tea Party in December 1773. Following the Civil War, the downtown of Boston became

more commercial and the church was threatened with demolition, but it was saved through the efforts of many Bostonians, among them Mary Porter Tileston Hemenway, who assisted in the formation of the Old South Preservation Committee, which owns the structure and operates it as a museum. On the far right is a corner of the *Boston Transcript* building, designed by Gridley J. Fox Bryant and built in 1873, where the largest daily newspaper in New England was published in quarto form in the late 19th century. The Old South Building was built in 1903 next to the Old South Church at 294 Washington Street. On the left is the Devenshire Towers, a high-rise apartment building designed by Steffian Bradley Associates and built in 1982. On the right is Exchange Place at 53 State Street, a high-rise tower designed by WZMH Group and built in 1981.

In 1873, the Old South Meeting House became a branch post office until the larger structure facing Post Office Square was completed. Adjacent to the Old South Meeting House is the immense Old South Building, which was built in 1903 as an office building at 294 Washington Street. Built in 1893, the Winthrop Building stands

to its left and was designed by Clarence Blackall. The Winthrop Building has a gentle curve, but its ornate overhanging cornice is its most impressive feature. Though dwarfing the old meeting house, it reinforces in our minds the importance of the events that once took place in its hallowed walls. Oliver Wendell Holmes said of it,

> Full sevenscore years our city's pride—
> The comely southern spire—
> Has cast its shadow, and defied
> The storm, the foe, the fire.

The area of lower Washington Street is today dominated by the Devonshire, a high-rise luxury apartment building with superb views of Boston. On the right is the former F. W. Woolworth's department store, which was built in 1965 at the corner of Washington and Franklin Streets and has become such stores as Marshall's, T. J. Maxx, the Boston Sports Club, and H&M. The Devonshire, on the left, and 60 State Street, on the right, flank the once prominent spire of the Old South Meeting House.

Photographed in 1857, Washington Street, south of Milk Street, was captured in the decade when the area was rapidly becoming more commercial. This area was adjacent to Cornhill, the section of Washington Street between Water and State Streets that had a large number of bookstores and newspaper publishers. In the center is the signboard of the old Washington Coffee House, a once fashionable boarding house and starting point in the early 19th century for the Groton and Leominster stagecoach. Named in 1789 for Pres. George Washington, it survived until 1855, after which it gave way to a multitude of commercial enterprises, including printing and engraving shops, shoe shops, haberdasheries, and dry goods stores. On the left is the old *Boston Transcript* building, while on the far right is the former F.W. Woolworth department store at the corner of Franklin Street, which

has now been remodeled for numerous stores on its first floor, with the parking garage remaining above.

Washington and Franklin Streets had a streetscape of commercial buildings, among them the Macullar, Williams & Parker Clothing Manufactory, which had been founded in 1849 and can be seen just to the right of the large awning in the center of the photograph. This manufactory was one of the best-known in New England as manufacturers of ready-made clothing. The white marble façade, which was only 50-feet wide for a vast building that extended 225 feet to Hawley Street, was a copy of the original that was destroyed by the Great Boston Fire of 1872. In the late 19th century, there were over 450 women and girls employed here, as well as 100 men. It was said that the employment was fair and equitable and that no "pinched or starved faces are seen" here. Today, the streetscape has become a modern addition to Filene's department store, which extends along Washington Street towards Franklin Street with an attractive sitting area at the corner that slopes down Franklin Street.

The Boston Court House was an impressive octagonal pavilion with flanking wings and a belfry surmounting the roof. It was designed by Charles Bulfinch and built in 1810 of Chelmsford granite. After 1840, the building was used as Boston City Hall until 1862, when the foundations for a new city hall were laid. It was also used as the first site of the Boston Public Library after its organization in 1843, with the donation of books from M. Alexandre Vattemare of Paris. The library would be officially founded in 1854. The city hall was once referred to as Johnson Hall in honor of Isaac and Lady Arbella Johnson, who owned the land in 1630 after arriving in America with John Winthrop. When the city hall was built, between 1862 and 1865, it was set back from School Street with a forecourt that had handsome quoined piers on School Street with

an impressive cast-iron gate. Today, the forecourt has statues and bronzes, as well as plantings that create an inviting area, especially during the summer months.

Boston City Hall was designed by Gridley J. Fox Bryant and Arthur Gilman and built between 1862 and 1865 on the site of the old courthouse at the corner of School Street and City Hall Avenue. An impressive building with a Louvre-inspired dome surmounted by a winged eagle, it is in the Italian Renaissance style of architecture "as modified and elaborated by modern French architects." White Concord granite was used on its façade, but the sides facing Court Square and City Hall Avenue are faced with the Chelmsford granite that was prudently and economically reused from the old courthouse. From the top of the copper dome rose a 200-foot flagstaff that at one time could be seen from most parts of the city before high-rise buildings were erected. In front of the old city hall are statues of Benjamin Franklin (1706–1790) on the left, sculpted by Richard Saltonstall Greenough, and Josiah Quincy (1772–1864), sculpted by Thomas Ball. Today, the old city hall has been renovated for offices with the popular restaurant Maison Robert on its first floor and Ben's Cafe in the basement.

Looking up School Street towards Tremont Street, the open area on the right is the forecourt of Boston City Hall, with City Hall Avenue on the far right. On the left are an office building at 44 School Street and the Parker House Hotel, which was later replaced by the present building designed by G. Henri Desmond and built in 1927. A corner of the Tremont Building, designed by Winslow & Wetherall, can be seen at the corner of Tremont and Beacon Streets. Just visible on the right is the Albion Building rising high above the roof of King's Chapel. The Old City Hall became superfluous after the present city hall was built in 1967, and the building was renovated in 1971 by Anderson, Notter Associates in 1969. It now has numerous offices, as well as the Maison Robert restaurant in the former city building.

Originally the site of the Haymarket from 1657 to 1711, which was on the open first floor of the Boston Town House, the Old State House was used as Boston City Hall by 1828, when a columned portico was added to the façade. Built in 1712, it served as the seat of the province's Colonial government until the American Revolution, when the symbols of royal governance, the gold-leafed coroneted lion and the silver-leafed unicorn, were ripped down and burned in front of the building on the site of the Boston Massacre as signs of British oppression. On the right is the colonnade of the United States Bank, which was designed by Isaiah Rogers. The Old State House, after numerous incarnations and having been sheathed in billboards and advertisements, was restored in 1881 and became the headquarters of the Bostonian Society. On the left is the Worthington Building at 31 State Street with the National Park Service Visitors Center and One State Street to the right. The Mellon Financial Center, designed by Pietro Belluschi, almost dwarfs the Colonial building, and to the right is One Beacon Street. As Henry Wadsworth Longfellow once said of the Old State House,

> Through days of sorrow and of mirth,
> Through days of death and days
>   of birth,
> Through every swift vicissitude
> Of changeful time, unchanged it
>   has stood.

The Old State House had been
remodeled by Isaiah Rogers in 1830
with a porch facing Congress Street
that was supported by paired columns.
Following the building in 1865 of Boston
City Hall, the building was used for a
number of purposes. The large number
of signs posted to its exterior shows
how many businesses were located here,
some of which were United States
Telegraph Company, Reed & Brother
Fire & Life Insurance, North American
Fire Insurance, and Smith & Company
Clothing Warerooms. The building was
saved from an ignoble fate, due mainly

to the efforts of William H. Whittemore,
then Boston city registrar and first
president of the newly founded Bostonian
Society, when it was restored by Boston
city architect George A. Clough in 1881.
Today, though the Old State House is a
museum dedicated to the preservation
and display of Boston's historical past,
the basement is used as a stop on the
Blue Line of the Massachusetts Bay
Transit Authority, which is convenient
for tourists headed for the visitors center
of the National Park Service at 15 State
Street, located to the left of the Old
State House.

Looking down State Street from Congress Street, the Merchants Exchange is on the right. Designed by Isaiah Rogers and built in 1842 for the Boston Board of Trade, this Greek Revival building had six engaged Corinthian pilasters, which were each 45-feet high and weighed 55 tons, supporting a pediment. The granite façade was severely plain, but carved lintels with amphimion detailing and a carved granite panel above the entrance of a globe surmounted by an eagle created interest. In addition to serving as the financial center of the city, the exchange was also the site of the post office until it moved to Post Office Square in 1873. The façade of 53 State Street, the former State Street Exchange designed by Peabody & Stearns, was fortunately saved through the intervention of local preservationists and maintains the quality of the late-19th-century streetscape. Just beyond the State Street Exchange can be seen 75 State Street, designed by Graham Gund Associates, and the Custom House Tower.

L ooking up State Street towards the Old State House from India Street, the area had become the financial district for Boston. On the right can be seen one of the two Queen Anne façade oriels of the Richards Building, which was a four-story cast-iron building manufactured in Italy that had two further stories added in the 1880s. State Street, by the late 19th century, had the Globe National Bank at 92, the Boston or State Street Exchange at 53, the Travelers Insurance Company of Hartford, the State National Bank at 40, the Third National Bank, the American Loan and Trust Company and the State Street Bank and Trust Company at 53, and the Market National Bank at 88. These banking institutions and insurance companies led to

State Street becoming an important part of Boston's financial economy.

The impressive State Street Exchange was designed by the noted architectural firm of Peabody & Stearns and built in 1891 on the site of the old Greek Revival Merchants Exchange on State Street between Kilby and Congress Streets. State Street in the early 19th century was often referred to as the Exchange, in imitation to London, where the businessmen of the city met daily to make transactions. As a result, here was located the home of the Boston Stock Exchange. Today, the restored rough-hewn granite façade of the building is part of Exchange Place, which is a modern high-rise office building of sleek glass that was designed by the architectural firm of WZMH Group and built in 1981. On the left is 75 State Street, designed by Graham Gund Architects and Skidmore, Owings & Merrill and built in 1988.

Boston has always been referred to as a "city upon a hill." In this early-19th-century print of Boston, as seen from Dorchester Heights in South Boston, the city was densely built up, with the Massachusetts State House prominently sited on the remaining portion of Beacon Hill at the time of Boston's incorporation as a city in 1822. The "Trimount" of Boston had seen the three hills—Mount Vernon, Beacon, and Pemberton Hills—reduced in size in the early 19th century, with the land being used to infill the flat of Beacon Hill and the graded lands developed for fashionable residential neighborhoods. In the foreground, a group of friends enjoy the panoramic vistas seen from the highest point in South Boston, which was annexed from Dorchester to Boston in 1804 and is today the site of the Dorchester Heights Evacuation Monument, which was designed by Peabody & Stearns and built in 1901.

Chapter 6

ALONG THE WATERFRONT: FINANCIAL DISTRICT

Looking north on Summer Street from Church Green in 1890, the street had been completely rebuilt after everything in the vicinity was destroyed by the Great Boston Fire of 1872. In 1873, the first Boston city architect was George A. Clough, who began to rebuild the city in a systematic approach with high-rise buildings set along the cleared and widened streets. On the left is the Church Green Building at the corner of Bedford and Summer Streets, which was thought to have been designed by Jonathan Preston. It is also thought to be the post–1877 location of the Shoe and Leather Exchange that was established in 1871 for the "purpose of promoting the general welfare of the hide and leather and boot and shoe interests of New England." At the corner of Summer and Devenshire Streets, on the right, is the Manufacturers National Bank, which was built in 1873, but was to survive less than four decades before it was demolished and a new building constructed. In the distance can be seen the spire of the Park Street Church, rising high above the buildings at Washington and Winter Streets in what is today referred to as Downtown Crossing.

Church Green in 1915 had changed in less than three decades with the Regal Shoe building on the left and the two-storied Corinthian columned Commonwealth Trust Company on the right, which was built on the site of the former Manufacturers National Bank at the corner of Summer and Devonshire Streets. In the distance can be seen the high-rise Gilchrist department store. Opened in 1842 at the corner of Washington and Winter Streets, Gilchrist's is one of numerous department stores, such as C.H. Hovey's, R.H. White's, and Kennedy's, that are now but a memory with only Filene's and Macy's (formerly Jordan Marsh & Company) surviving. Notice the E. Howard & Company street clock in the foreground, which was one of many that were placed throughout the city and its neighborhoods. Today, rising high above the Church Green Building is 99 Summer Street, a high-rise stepped office building designed by Goody, Clancy & Associates and built in 1986.

S ummer Street, looking south from Washington Street, was a busy thoroughfare with streetcars seemingly lined up for blocks along the entire street, almost all of which was rebuilt in 1873 and 1874. On the left is Noyes Brothers Golf Store at the corner of Otis Street, and on the right is the Merchants Building at the corner of Kingston Street. Today, Summer Street is dominated by Filene's and Macy's department stores, as well as numerous office buildings and stores. In the distance is 125 Summer Street, designed by Kohn, Pederson, Fox and built in 1990 above a streetscape of post–Great Boston Fire buildings that wrap around the base of the tower and maintain the late-Victorian scale of the streetscape with a high-rise above.

The Boston Post Office and Sub-Treasury survived the Great Boston Fire of 1872. Built on Congress Street between Milk and Water Streets, this impressive Cape Ann granite Renaissance-style building was designed by A.A. Mullett in association with subarchitects Gridley J. Fox Bryant and Alexander R. Esty and completed in 1875. The 200-foot façade is adorned with two marble groups sculpted by Daniel Chester French (1850–1931). On the left is *Labor*, representing a stalwart figure with "his right arm supported by the horn of the anvil against which he is leaning," with a mother and child under his muscled arm. *Fine Arts* is represented by "a graceful woman supporting a vase on her knee, with sculptured masks and capitals lying at her feet." On the right is *Science*, which is portrayed as "a woman seated in the middle directing *Electricity*, a youth with winged feet, as she rests with her left hand on the shoulder of *Steam*, who is chained to a locomotive wheel. *Science* rests her foot on a closed volume,–her undiscovered secrets,– and supports on her left arm a horseshoe magnet with a thunderbolt as an armature." The current Art Deco post office was designed by Cram and Ferguson

in 1929. In the foreground, in Angell Memorial Park, designed by Earl Flansburgh and Associates, is a monument designed by Peabody and Stearns and erected to the memory of George Thorndike Angell, founder of the Massachusetts Society for the Prevention of Cruelty to Animals and public benefactor of the society, which did much to lessen the suffering of all animals, especially those involved with horse street railways—or the horse-drawn carriage seen in the foreground!

The south side of Post Office Square on Milk Street between Pearl and Congress Streets had the Mutual Life Insurance Company of New York and the New England Mutual Life Insurance Company. Designed by Nathaniel J. Bradlee (1829–1888) of the noted Boston architectural firm of Bradlee, Winslow

& Wetherall, and built of white marble in 1874, the New England Mutual Life Insurance Company shares similar architectural details of an emblematic bronze group on the roof parapet with its neighboring life insurance company. The Mutual Life Insurance Company of New York, however, was designed by Peabody & Stearns with a soaring clock tower punctuating the mansard roof, gilded crests, and an iron flagstaff. Each was five stories in height with fanciful Renaissance Revival details and iron mansard roofs. Interestingly, the basement was the first location of the Boston Safe Deposit and Trust Company. The stepped Art Deco telephone headquarters was designed by Cram & Ferguson and built in 1947 on the site of the insurance buildings. The lush and inviting park at Post Office Square was designed by the Halvorson Company, a landscape architectural firm, and Ellenzweig Associates, architects who created an oasis in the center of Post Office Square with the ever useful and highly utilized multi-level parking garage located underground.

The tower of the Mutual Life Insurance Company of New York was designed by Peabody and Stearns and built in 1875 with a four-sided clock that could be seen from any point in Post Office Square. The clock also offered from its balcony just below the roof cap one of the most breathtaking views of Boston. The clock's four dials were actually ten feet and six inches in diameter and were strategically placed on the 234-foot marble tower that had an impressive gilded balcony, which caught the sun and became a beacon. On the left is a corner of the Converse Building at Milk and Pearl Streets. Today, the State Street Bank is on the left, and the Keystone Building at 99 High Street on the right.

M ilk Street, looking towards Washington Street, had impressive buildings constructed after the Great Boston Fire of 1872 that represented the epitome of late-Victorian architecture. Here, the Goddard Building, designed by

Nathaniel J. Bradlee and William Winslow, and the *Boston Post* building to the right, designed by Peabody and Stearns, are draped with bunting and decorations for the nation's centennial observances in 1875. The *Boston Post* building had been built on the site of Benjamin Franklin's birthplace and childhood home (notice a small bust of the printer and philanthropist above the second floor) and is now the General Bank. The Centennial Lunch Room, which provided hot and hopefully nutritious lunches to city workers can be seen on the far left. Today, Franklin's birthplace, which was destroyed by a fire in 1810, is One Milk Street, the headquarters of the International Institute of Boston and the Immigrant Museum's well-presented multimedia show *Dreams of Freedom*.

In a view looking down Milk Street from Washington Street in 1890, the ivy clad side of the Old South Meeting House can be seen on the left, as well as the buildings along the west side of Milk Street, all of which were built after 1873. The tall building in the distance, rising above the roof of the Old South Church, is the elegant Equitable Life Assurance Society of New York, which was also the headquarters of some leading legal firms and many of the wealthiest corporations and individuals in Boston in the late 19th century. On its roof was originally a time-ball that would daily drop at noon, serving as a regulator for clocks, watches, and timepieces in the area, as well as a local version of the more well-known Greenwich, England, time ball that drops at 1:00 p.m. daily. The buildings at

45 Milk Street and 31 Milk Street are in the center, as the street curves towards Liberty Square.

Jordan Marsh & Company was the largest department store in New England at the turn of the 20th century. A vast building, bound by Washington, Avon, and Summer Streets, it was designed by the Boston architectural firm of Winslow & Wetherall and had a total of 66 departments, 3,500 employees, and 15 acres of floor space in 1895. The store was founded in 1841 by Eben Dyer Jordan and his partner, Benjamin L. Marsh. They were considered pioneers in modern methods of merchandising and generous and benevolent gentlemen who supported numerous local charities and worthy causes. Although many older Bostonians still defiantly refer to the store as Jordan Marsh, it has actually been a branch of Macy's since 1996. Macy's had been founded by Rowland Hussey Macy, a native of Nantucket who opened his first store in Manhattan. On the right is the Corner, a group of shops located in the former Gilchrist department store, which was closed in 1977.

Filene's department store was designed by the Chicago architect Daniel Burnham and built in 1911 at the corner of Washington and Summer Streets. William Filene had opened his first store in Salem in 1852, later moving to Boston in 1881. He commissioned an eight-story department store, with its façade of gray and olive green terra cotta that creates an interesting coloration to the streetscape. Filene established his store in Boston as a progressive retail, employee-owned corporation that also instituted the now often taken for granted profit sharing, which hopefully propelled employees to excel in annual sales. The store had a rooftop recreation field, an employee hospital, a library, and a meeting hall, in addition to a fine dining room for shoppers. The high-rise office building is 101 Arch Street, which was designed by Hoskins Scott Taylor & Partners and built in 1989 behind the façade of the old Kennedy's department store and post–1873 buildings on Arch Street.

The Albion Building, designed by Cummings and Sears and built in 1888, stood at the corner of Tremont and Beacon Streets, and was home to the once famous Houghton & Dutton department store. On the lower left can be seen the upper corner of the Tremont House, Boston's first luxury hotel, which was built in 1829 and demolished in 1895. Today, a corner of the Tremont Building can be seen on the left, along with a corner of One Beacon Place, which was designed by Skidmore, Owings & Merrill and built in 1972, and a portion of Center Plaza.

The Ames Building was designed by the Boston architectural firm of Shepley, Rutan & Coolidge and built in 1892 as an investment for the Ames family at the corner of Court and Washington Streets. An impressive building with repetitive Romanesque Revival arches along the façades, it was 190 feet high, but is currently vacant and awaiting a new tenant. In the foreground is the Sears Building, which was a Ruskinian Gothic building built in 1868 and which had the first elevator in Boston. It is now the site of the Mellon Financial Center, formerly the Boston Company building at One Boston Place, which was designed by Pietro Belluschi.

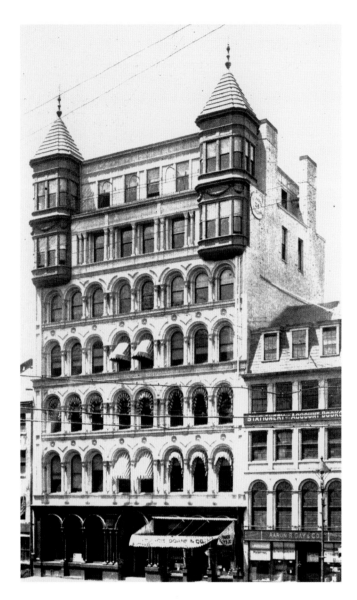

The Richards Building is the earliest surviving cast-iron building in Boston. Made with paired columns between arches, the four-storied façade was manufactured in Italy and only assembled when it arrived in Boston. Built just after the Civil War, it was in marked comparison to the buildings only recently built of hewn granite. In the 1880s, the building was enlarged with the addition of two stories that had fanciful Queen Anne-style oriels on the corners.

The impressive Boston Board of Trade building was built in 1915 on India Street between Milk and State Streets. The three arches with freestanding columns created a dramatic entrance, as did the limestone quoining and the detailed cornice. Established in 1854, the board was composed of merchants and businessmen "when the commercial interests of the city were at a low ebb, with the hope of concentrating its business energies and advancing enterprises to improve its commercial position." On the left can be seen a corner of the Boston Custom House, which was designed by Ammi Burnham Young and built between 1837 and 1849 of Quincy granite. The board of trade building is today still an elegant building, with numerous offices. On the left can be seen a corner of the Boston Custom House, and in the distance a portion of 75 State Street, designed by Graham Gund Associates, rises above the old board of trade building.

The State Street Trust Company was designed by the Boston architectural firm of Parker, Thomas & Rice and built on Congress Street at the corner of State Street, on the site of the Tremont National Bank. An elegant, classical design, the building sat adjacent to the Boston Stock Exchange at 53 State Street, occupying a broad façade facing Congress Street, but narrow on its sides. The interior was designed by Richardson, Barott & Richardson, which had impressive banking spaces that were elegantly appointed and filled with a fabulous collection of Boston- and marine-related items. The corner of the façade of the State Street Exchange can be seen on the left. It was saved when the interior was completely gutted and a modern structure was built in the early 1980s. The screen of glass facing Congress Street adds a distinctly modernistic aspect to the venerable building.

A view looking across the 40-acre Boston Common from the Little Building shows Tremont Street on the right as a bustling shopping area at the turn of the 20th century. Boston Common was laid out in 1634 as common ground, and is the oldest public park in the United States. The common is known for the frog pond and is embellished with many notable works of art, including the Soldiers and Sailors Civil War Monument by Martin Milmore, the Gardner Brewer Fountain, the Boston Massacre Monument, and the tablet dedicated to the first game of football played in Boston. In the foreground, at the corner of Boylston and Beacon Streets, are the kiosks designed by Edmund March Wheelwright for the first subway in the nation. The subway extended the length of Boylston Street from Park Street to Boylston Street and later continued along Boylston Street through the Back Bay. In the distance can be seen the spire of the Park Street Church, and on the left the prominent dome of the Massachusetts State House is seen.

Chapter 7

FROG LANE: LOWER BOYLSTON STREET

The Boylston Market was designed by Charles Bulfinch and built in 1809 at the corner of Washington and Boylston Streets for the Boylston Market Association. Named for the great philanthropist and donor of the four-sided cupola clock, Ward Nicholas Boylston (1749–1828), the market had stalls on the first floor and Boylston Hall above, which was the scene of many meetings, dramatic performances, and entertainment. It also had the performance space of the Handel and Hayden Society after 1817. The hall soon proved too small and was enlarged in 1859. Eleven years later, the entire building was moved eleven feet back from Washington Street to allow for street widening, all of which was for naught as the market was demolished in 1888. The cupola was placed on a brewery in Charlestown, after which it was placed on the Cavalry Methodist Church in suburban Arlington. In the distance can be seen the tower of the Young Men's Christian Union, designed by Nathaniel J. Bradlee and built in 1875, and the Hotel Touraine just beyond at the corner of Tremont Street. Today, the Romanesque Revival-style Boylston Building, designed by Carl Fehmer and built in 1888, stands on the site of the old Boylston Market and is known as the China Trade Center.

Colonnade Row was a streetscape of 19 row houses designed by Charles Bulfinch and built in 1811 on Tremont Street between West and Mason Streets. These row houses, like the Tontine Crescent on Franklin Street and those on Park Street, changed the architectural style of Boston. The city saw the building of entire streetscapes of connected row houses with cast-iron balconies extending along the second floor, or piano nobile, as it was referred to. These fashionable houses faced the Lafayette Mall, named for the Marquis de La Fayette, which was a promenade along the edge of the Boston Common in the two decades prior to the Civil War. In 1903, a large office building replaced the former Lawrence House at the corner of Tremont and West Streets that has today been converted into the Suffolk College Residence Hall. In the 1960s, the high-rise Tremont on the Common was

built at 151 Tremont Street, which is today luxury condominiums with superb views overlooking Boston Common, as well as the equally elegant condominiums at the Parkside at 170 Tremont Street .

The Masonic Temple was designed by local architect Merrill G. Wheelock and built in 1867 at the corner of Tremont and Boylston Streets. An impressive Gothic design granite building, it had twin octagonal towers on the façade corners that spanned to 120 feet with pinnacles rising above. In the 19th century, the first floor was rented out to Ivers & Pond Piano Company and the Home Savings Bank, with the remainder of the building used for the numerous Masonic organizations of the city. The temple had three large meeting halls, one furnished in the Corinthian style, another in the Egyptian, and the third in the Gothic, as well as a large Masonic library. The present Masonic Temple, an impressive limestone building, was designed by the Boston architectural firm of Loring & Phipps and built in 1899 as the headquarters of the Grand Lodge of Massachusetts and 13 other Blue Lodges. Rising high above the Masonic Temple are the new high-rise condominiums known as the Residences of the Ritz Carlton Hotel.

The Boston Public Library was designed by Charles Kirby and built in 1858 on Boylston Street, opposite the Boston Common and the Deer Park. Founded in 1854, the Boston Public Library was the largest public library in 19th-century America, second only to that of the Library of Congress. First librarian Edward Capen was later followed by Charles Coffin Jewett, who served as librarian from 1857–1868. The library was built of red brick and sandstone, and had heavily quoined corners and an arched rusticated entrance with heavily detailed arched windows on its façade. As Boston expanded, so too did the library, and the first branch library in the United States was established in 1870 in East Boston. The library survived just over four decades, being demolished in 1899 after the McKim, Mead and White library was built in Copley Square. Today, the site of the old Boston Public Library

is that of the Colonial Building, which has the opulently appointed Colonial Theatre on the first floor and offices above. On its left is the Little Building, which is now part of Emerson College and used as a dormitory.

Tremont Street, near Boylston Street, had on its left the Aeolian Organ Company and the Haines Brothers Piano Company in the American Protective League building. On its right was the Ivers & Pond Piano Company and the Home Savings Bank in the Masonic Temple building. This area of Tremont Street had a large number of showrooms that offered musical instruments manufactured both locally and abroad. A Boston & Chelsea streetcar travels south on Tremont Street and a portion of the late-Victorian cast-iron railing enclosing Boston Common can be seen in the foreground. Today, the block between Mason and Boylston Streets includes the new Loews Theatres, the Residences of the Ritz Carlton Towers, Action for Boston Community Development (ABCD), the Urban College of Boston, and Emerson College and its Radio WERS. The Masonic Temple is still located at the corner of Tremont and Boylston Streets. In the foreground is the limestone kiosk designed by Edmund March Wheelwright for the Inbound trolley at Boylston/Theatre District Station.

The Little Building is an imposing modified Gothic office building that was jointly designed by the architectural firms of Blackall, Clapp & Whittemore and Little & Russell and built in 1926 at the corner of Boylston and Tremont Streets. Often referred to as a virtual "city under one roof," the numerous specialty shops on the first two floors offered not just convenience for office workers in the building, but inside shopping on inclement weather days. The Little Building was a 12-story office building with octagonal recessed windows set between vertical pilasters, and it had a large sign advertising for "Little Building" that was mounted on the roof and could be seen from across Boston Common. Today, the Little Building is owned by Emerson College and is used as a dormitory, which has superb views across the Boston Common. On the right can be seen a corner of the Colonial Building.

Bowdoin Square, looking from the Bowdoin Square Garage, was the junction of Cambridge, Bowdoin, and Green Streets. Seen in a photograph of the early 1920s, the area was part of the old West End of Boston and was a densely built up vicinity of hotels, movie houses, places of entertainment, and commercial businesses coexisting in a section that extended from Bowdoin Square to Scollay Square. Towering high above the intersection is the Peabody & Stearns designed Custom House tower with its impressive four-sided clock, which has been renovated as the Marriott Custom House. Today, on the far left is the art deco Verizon telephone building with Boston City Hall Plaza and the John Fitzgerald Kennedy federal building to its right. To the right of Bowdoin Square is the Leverett Saltonstall Building, built in 1967, at the corner of Bowdoin Street.

Acknowledgments

We would like to thank the following who contributed either directly or indirectly in the research, writing, and editing of this photographic history: Jill Anderson, Richard M. Candee, Frank Cheney, Elise Cirgna, Dexter, Mary Kyprianos Ducas, Edward W. Gordon, Helen Hannon, Rev. Michael J. Parise, Joseph Lo Piccolo, Susan Wood Paine, J.B. Price, Anthony and Mary Mitchell Sammarco, William Varrell, the New England Chapter of the Victorian Society, and Virginia M. White.

Bacon's Dictionary of Boston, edited by Edwin M. Bacon and published in 1883, and the *AIA Guide to Boston* by Susan and Michael Southworth have proved invaluable in researching and writing this book. Unless specified differently, all quotes used in the text are from Bacon's book.

Unless otherwise noted, "then" photographs are from the collection of Anthony M. Sammarco, and "now" photographs were taken by James Z. Kyprianos.

"A city's future is but a logical extension of its past."

—John F. Collins, former mayor of Boston